J. CRAIG ANNAN

WILLIAM BUCHANAN

THE ART OF
THE PHOTOGRAPHER
J. CRAIG ANNAN
1864–1946

NATIONAL GALLERIES OF SCOTLAND
1992

Published by the Trustees of the National Galleries of Scotland
for the exhibition *The Art of the Photographer: J. Craig Annan*
at the Scottish National Gallery of Modern Art
14 August to 11 October 1992

CONTENTS

FOREWORD

James Craig Annan is a major figure in the history of photography and it is appropriate that this evaluation of his role should be carried out by William Buchanan who has spent many years studying his work. At the turn of the century Annan was a part of the vital artistic life of Glasgow when photography took its place easily with the other fine arts. His work was innovative and his exploration of the possibilities of the photogravure process raised the whole question of the apparent opposition between the instantaneous reaction of the camera to subject matter and the manipulation of the image after it had been made.

¶ Annan's work had a profound effect on the American photographer Alfred Stieglitz and they were to remain in contact until the mid-1940s. By this time Annan had long given up photography and the art itself had to struggle for some of the credibility it had had without question at the beginning of the century. Stieglitz's high regard for Annan is an indication of the seminal influence the Glasgow photographer undoubtedly had in the worldwide development of art photography in these years and we are certain that the time is now more than ripe for a reconsideration of the subtleties and beauty of the work of this very considerable Scottish artist.

TIMOTHY CLIFFORD   *Director, National Galleries of Scotland*

DUNCAN THOMSON *Keeper, Scottish National Portrait Gallery*

ACKNOWLEDGEMENTS

We gratefully acknowledge the essential help of T. & R. Annan & Sons Ltd., Glasgow, through John C. Annan and Douglas M. Annan, the fourth and fifth generations from J. Craig Annan's elder brother John.

¶ The following institutions kindly gave their help: Aberdeen Art Gallery, Francina Irwin; Christie's London, Lindsey Stewart; Edinburgh Photographic Society, James Castel; Glasgow Art Gallery and Museum, Celine Blair and Hugh Stevenson; Glasgow School of Art, Ian Monie and Peter Trowles; Glasgow University Library, Dr Nigel Thorp; Hamilton Libraries & Museum, Isabel Walker; Hunterian Art Gallery, Glasgow University, Martin Hopkinson and Pamela Robertson; Mitchell Library Glasgow, Staffs of Arts Music and Recreation, Photography and Rare Books Departments; National Library of Scotland, Richard Ovenden; National Museum of Photography, Film and Television, Bradford, Julian Cox and Roger Taylor; Royal Photographic Society Bath, Pamela Roberts and Gill Thompson; Stirling Central Library, Allan Jeffrey.

¶ The following individuals gave generously of their specialist skills: Bruce Bernstein, Marion Breen, Rob Burnet, Karen Moon, Stephen Mulrine, Michael Roschlau and Anne Stewart.

¶ At the Scottish National Portrait Gallery I wish to record my thanks to Alexandra Aikman and Julie Lawson and especially to the Curator of Photography, Sara Stevenson, for their help with the preparation of this text. Sara Stevenson's formidable scholarship, especially of the work of Hill and Adamson (admired and championed by Annan) is an inspiration to the few but growing number of scholars picking at the rich vein of Scottish Photography.

WILLIAM BUCHANAN

J. CRAIG ANNAN

§ PICTORIALISM

At the beginning of the last decade of the 19th century photography began a battle for recognition as an art in its own right. Campaigns rumbled first throughout Europe and then the United States of America until the end of the first decade of the 20th century. Pitched battles – international exhibitions of photography, at which James Craig Annan was often present – broke out in Vienna in 1891, London and Hamburg in 1893 and Paris in 1894. They spread as far as Russia. In the United States early shots were fired in 1898 in Philadelphia and in 1899 in Newark. In 1910 Annan was invited to exhibit in 'The International Exhibition of Pictorial Photography' at Buffalo, a victory parade. In Glasgow, Annan's home, warning shots went off in 1891 and its exhibition of 1897 was but the prelude for a global set-to in 1901. Photography's regiments marched in all shapes and sizes. From Hamburg came *Die Gesellschaft zur Förderung der Amateur-Photographie* (The Society for the Advancement of Amateur Photography), from London the Linked Ring Brotherhood, from New York the Photo-Secession, from Vienna *Das Kleeblatt* (The Trefoil). There was the *Photo-Club de Paris* and the Photographic Society of Philadelphia and many others.

¶ Medals were awarded for excellence in the brave art of photography. Annan collected more than most: from Austria, Belgium (fig.2), France, Germany, Hungary, India, Italy, the Netherlands, Russia and Scotland. Little wonder, when the photographers attempted to form the International Society of Pictorial Photographers in 1904, that it was Annan who was approached to be its President. Annan's work was a yardstick against which others were measured. In 1895 Alfred Stieglitz complained about the standard of artistic photography in the United States, 'We have no Robinsons, Sutcliffes, Annans.'[1] In 1898 Robert Demachy wrote about conditions in France, 'We have no men like Craig Annan, Crooke or Hollyer.'[2] In Germany in 1900 Ernst Juhl measured progress by noting, 'It was only a few years ago that there were no professional photographers possessed of the artistic aims shown by Craig Annan, Hollyer etc.'[3] To disparage the first Philadelphia Photographic Salon in 1898 all that was needed was to indicate 'in the A's of the catalogue there are only two names, and that of J. Craig Annan is not one of them.'[4]

FIG. 1
J. Craig Annan *c.1895*
by Alexander Roche
Modern print
Scottish National Portrait
Gallery, Edinburgh

[9

FIG. 2
Medal
by I. S. De Rudder
Inscribed 'L'Effort A. M.
Annam (sic) 1902'
*L'Effort, founded in 1900, was
a secessionist group from the*
Association Belge de
Photographie. *It held Salons in
Brussels from 1901 to 1905.
T. & R. Annan & Sons Ltd.,
Glasgow*

¶ Annan's work was used as ammunition. 'It is not necessary to talk about superiority, equality, or inferiority in comparing photography with other arts. Mr Annan's portraits fulfill an artistic intention and are therefore complete in themselves.'[5] Again, 'our exhibitions of painting show mastery quite inferior to that of Annan, Crooke, Hollyer, Furley Lewis, Hoppé, and several other British workers – not to mention many in other countries.'[6] Annan's work appeared in many publications, such as *The Studio* or *Photograms of the Year*, both published in London. It was beautifully reproduced in *Die Kunst in der Photographie* first published in Berlin, in *Photographische Rundschau* published in Halle, in *Photographisches Centralblatt* and *Wiener Photographische Blätter*, both published in Vienna, in the de luxe editions of the catalogues of the *Photo-Club de Paris* and in *Camera Notes* and *Camera Work* of New York.

¶ The key protagonists bought his prints: in Hamburg, Ernst Juhl, and Alfred Lichtwark for the Kunsthalle; in Munich, Fritz Matthies-Masuren; in Dresden, Max Lehrs for the Kupferstich-Kabinett; and in New York by Stieglitz whose collection is now mainly in the Metropolitan Museum of Art. At Buffalo in 1910, the Albright Gallery purchased *The Lombardy Ploughing Team*. The rare private collectors also purchased. In 1894 Harold Holcroft from Wolverhampton bought *The Lombardy Ploughing Team, Franciscan of Il Redentore* and *Janet Burnet*. The collection of George Timmins of Syracuse, New York, formed in the early part of the 1890s, has now disappeared but it contained *The Lombardy Ploughing Team, A Little Princess, Sybilla* and *Fisherwives*.

¶ The dizziest panegyrics were heaped on Annan. *The Lombardy Ploughing Team* was, in 1900, 'too perfect a thing of its kind to call for any criticism.'[7] *The Ruined Castle (Harlech Castle)* was, in 1909, 'one of those renderings of a subject that makes one feel that no one else ought to touch it.'[8] Even *Janet Burnet*, 'one of the classics of photography' to quote from Annan's obituary[9], was surpassed by *The White Friars*, 'one of the greatest pictures ever made by means of the camera.'[10] At the end of last century Annan was 'universally conceded, by all competent judges, to be one of the ablest, the most gifted, most artistic of the really great pictorial photographic leaders of the times.'[11] Yet interest in him vanished after a real war in 1914. Was he a much decorated but hollow hero?

¶ At the end of this century, to eyes accustomed to Diane Arbus's disturbing work, or to the chilling carnage in Don McCullin, the Pictorialists appear, at worst, affected and arty, with photographs mimicking oil paintings, idealised sheep in smudgy landscapes, fuzzy, overly posed nudes – one daintily skipping while a-clashing cymbals. There is no denying their occasional preciousness. Nevertheless, these are works of the greatest delicacy and subtlety, printed often in carbon or photogravure, with high skill, on translucent Japanese papers. Uppermost in the minds of their creators was that difficult concept, beauty (this does not deny beauty in Arbus or McCullin). While it is interesting that Annan's *The White Friars* was rated so highly in 1900, what is its status and that of the rest of his work almost a hundred years on?

§ EDUCATION

'Mr Craig Annan may be said to have inhaled a photographic and artistic atmosphere from childhood, and in a metaphorical sense to have been cradled among *materia photographica*.'[12] Even the place of his birth, on 8 March 1864, had a photographic reference. Talbot Cottage is at 15 Burnbank Road, Hamilton, about 10 miles to the south west of Glasgow.

¶ His father, Thomas Annan (1829–87), was one of the most important nineteenth-century photographers. In addition to setting up a thriving commercial business, he succeeded in taking photographs of considerable orginality. His *Old Closes and Streets of Glasgow*, by which he is best remembered, is a powerful and moving essay on the condemned slums of the city. He also proved himself a distinguished landscape and portrait photographer. His photograph of the explorer David Livingstone (fig. 3), taken when James was about six months old, is one of the memorable portraits of its century.[13]

FIG. 3
David Livingstone *1864*
by Thomas Annan
Carbon
Scottish National Portrait Gallery, Edinburgh

[11

FIG. 4
D. O. Hill *c.1867*
by Thomas Annan
Carbon
From Calotypes by D. O. Hill
& Robert Adamson Selected
from his collection by Andrew
Elliot *printed for private
circulation, Edinburgh, 1928.*
*Scottish National Portrait
Gallery, Edinburgh*

¶ In 1865 the painter and photographer, David Octavius Hill (fig. 4) came with his wife to stay at Talbot Cottage. There Hill put the final touches to his long unfinished painting 'Signing the Act of Separation', showing the secession of the Free Church of Scotland. James was told later by his elder brother that their father had photographed the painting in the open air. To reproduce this work, Thomas Annan chose Joseph Swan's permanent carbon process, giving the company its first major order. That year Thomas purchased the rights for Swan's process in Scotland, an important acquisition as the firm specialised in the reproduction of works of art. Perhaps it was at D. O. Hill's wish that the Annan family moved in 1869 into Rock House in Edinburgh where Hill and Adamson had taken their superb calotype photographs twenty-five years previously. This time James was old enough to recall meeting the venerable Hill who gave him a pencil and sheet of paper and set him to draw. However, the Annans stayed only six months. After Hill's death in 1870, his widow presented Thomas with ninety calotypes which he bound into two volumes.[14] James recalled that he looked at them as a schoolboy, so there should be no surprise to catch resonances of Hill and Adamson in his work.

¶ In November 1877 Thomas Annan moved to Lenzie, about six miles north-east of the smoke of Glasgow, to set up a carbon printing establishment. He built on ground at Beechmount Road where a correspondent for *The British Journal of Photography*[15] saw, in 1878, 3,000 prints made for his published edition of *Old Closes and Streets of Glasgow*. The firm became one of the three biggest producers of carbon tissue in Britain. Both James and his elder brother were already helping their father. James had left Hamilton Academy when he was thirteen, but in 1878–9 he extended his knowledge of chemistry by attending lectures at Anderson's College.

¶ Thomas Annan's interest was next aroused in photogravure, another fine permanent process. The first example in Britain was a portrait of Mungo Ponton which appeared in the *Yearbook of Photography* in 1882. By February 1883 James was travelling with his father to Vienna to learn the secret process from Karl Klíč who had invented it four years before. From Thomas's letters[16] it is possible to reconstruct their visit. They arrived in Vienna on Saturday 24 February. They met Klíč at his *Photochemische Werkstätten* in the Belvederegasse 22. Thomas noticed that Klíč suffered from headaches but was full of humour. 'I take him to be a genuine simple minded enthusiastic genius.'[17] An agreement was drawn up that James would be taught the process for 2,500 Austrian florins. The Annans had brought a negative (the largest size Klíč had tried) of Joseph Noel Paton's minutely worked *The Fairy Raid*. On 6 March they were still working on the plate. Nevertheless, they saw the old masters in the Belvedere nearby and Klíč gave them a fine dinner of fish from the Danube with Hungarian wine. At the end of the meal Klíč enjoyed, with nips of brandy, Annan's Scottish proverbs though they must have lost a lot in translation. On the 8 March James became nineteen and on the 14th their business was complete. They left with James's 'prentice piece – the photogravure plate of *The Fairy Raid* – and an agreement that its prints could be exhibited as his own work, and the purchase of the rights of Klíč's process for Great Britain and Ireland.

¶ James's father died on 14 December 1887. His obituary in *The British Journal of Photography* on 23 December recorded that he was 'Cultured . . . fastidious in taste', qualities which he bequeathed in full to his son James – together with his great height. Thomas Annan was remembered not for his own photographs, but 'the reproduction of paintings, obtaining for him wide and most honourable distinction.' For James, who in 1885 had gone to London to superint with Donald Swan a new firm of photo-engravers, Annan and Swan, at 7 Devonshire Road, the death of his father meant a return to Glasgow to become a partner in the firm and its 'practical photogravurist'. In the last years of the century Annan's became firmly established and financially secure. On 26 September 1889 T. & R. Annan & Sons received a Royal Warrant as 'Photographers and Photographic Engravers to her Majesty in Glasgow'. At some time about 1890 Annan decided to follow his own interests in photography. He may have been stimulated by making photogravure prints from Hill and Adamson's calotype negatives (plate 1). James Craig Annan's own character and appearance were unexpected for a man who was to achieve international celebrity. He was described as 'tall, precise and business-like and of a retiring disposition.'[18] *The Bailie* journal said he was 'of a modest and unassuming habit of mind and is greatly beloved by all who know him'.[19] He was a familiar figure at the Glasgow Art Club 'with his clean-shaven face – reminding one of a young monk.'[20] None of this implies the intensity of his photographic work or his immense influence and energy in the world of pictorial photography. He was both an introspective and a dynamic man.

¶ It may seem strange that Annan, who was to become a leader in art photography, had no formal training in fine art. He learned by making reproductions of works of art. In addition, the firm's premises at 153 Sauchiehall Street were used as fine art galleries, exhibiting paintings like John Everett Millais's *Christ in the House of His Parents*. The firm's specialisation in reproduction enabled him to have access to private collections, otherwise closed to the public. Most notably his work for the royal collection allowed him the privilege of studying the Holbeins at

FIG. 5
George Walton *c.1897*
Matt collodion
Scottish National Portrait Gallery, Edinburgh

Windsor. As a young man Annan's close friends were artists: the etchers D. Y. Cameron and William Strang, the sculptor Pittendrigh Macgillivray and the designer George Walton (fig. 5). He also knew most of the artists in the city which was experiencing a great outburst of creativity. When interviewed in 1896 about influences on his work he cited Japanese art, Whistler and Velázquez, the heroes of the leading Glasgow painters – the 'Glasgow Boys'.

¶ Glasgow's interest in photography was also a stimulus to him. At an exhibition there in 1886 he saw daguerreotypes, calotypes by W. H. F. Talbot in *The Pencil of Nature*, and by David Octavius Hill and Robert Adamson. He saw Julia Margaret Cameron's superb *Sir John Herschel* and Oscar Rejlanders's large *The Two Ways of Life*, a composite of thirty negatives. The two principal polemicists of art and photography exhibited: Henry Peach Robinson showed *Dawn and Sunset*, whose sentimentality may not have appealed to the 'Glasgow Boys'; Peter Henry Emerson's photograph of a working ploughman, *A Stiff Pull*, would teach Annan about blurring and movement. But there were no works listed by Annan himself although the firm contributed *A Fairy Raid* and *Objects of Vertu, Hamilton Palace Sale*.

¶ Annan emerged publicly as a photographer in 1891 when he joined the committee for the exhibition held by the Glasgow and West of Scotland Amateur Photographic Association. It attracted photographers from Austria, France, Germany, Russia and, among six from the United States, Stieglitz who showed *Professor Vogel, Maria Ballatti, Ernesto* and *Self-portrait*. Frustratingly, the catalogue gives one entry for Annan as *Hand Camera Pictures*, and both numbers 630 and 631 are *A Sculptor's Workshop*, untraced portraits of Macgillivray. It was the following year when his work began to make its impact on the world.

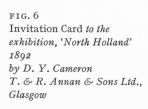

FIG. 6
Invitation Card *to the exhibition, 'North Holland' 1892*
by D. Y. Cameron
T. & R. Annan & Sons Ltd., Glasgow

§ NORTH HOLLAND, NORTH ITALY

In 1892 Annan, with D. Y. Cameron, toured North Holland. Annan was to notice that 'It has been when I have associated with artists that I have made my most successful pictures; when I have spent a holiday with others who had little intimate knowledge of art, I have found my camera to be sadly lacking in that subtle something which makes one photograph so very much more interesting than another.'[21] Annan was carrying out the advice he was to give to others. Go 'anywhere he can throw aside for the time his everyday mind which balances ledgers, worries about bills or rent, and with his holiday mind start fresh with but one idea – pictorial photography.'[22]

¶ The invitation to the exhibition 'North Holland' (fig.6) announced 'A series of etchings and monotones by D. Y. Cameron and J. Craig Annan'. Annan fought shy of using the word photograph, presumably not to inhibit people from considering his work on the same terms as the etchings. The exhibition was mounted in October 1892 in new premises at 230 Sauchiehall Street where Walton had designed the interior, furniture and frames (fig.7).[23] It was beautifully presented against cool greys and greens with the etchings and photographs hung together. Unusually, the photographs provided colour, for Annan had printed in red, green and brown.[24] Some were presented in square flat frames, like Dutch tiles. It was a bold approach. Annan had produced fresh and vital prints from the overworked subject matter found in the canvases of the Hague School. He arranged his fisher folk in the tiny *The Beach at Zandvoort* (plate 2), like notes of music, in a slanting line across the top of the print. *On a Dutch Shore* (plate 3) is assymetrically composed, the small dark rectangle formed by the group intent on a fish auction balanced against the shapes of two *pinken* (fishing boats). These two prints, in their abstract compositions, are undeniably modern. They are so-called art photographs, yet they also document vividly the lives of a people governed by the wind and the sea. Annan could not have stage-managed these scenes. He was exploiting the camera's ability to sieze the composition once the pieces fell into place.

¶ Through exhibition and reproduction these prints reached most people then interested in photography. Most importantly, a print of *The Road through the Sand Dunes* (plate 4) reached Stieglitz. Weston Naef has pointed out[25] that this was one of the works which influenced Stieglitz's style between 1894 and 1900. Stieglitz followed Annan's example and carried his camera onto a Netherlandish beach in 1894: his *Landing of the Boats* shows another crucial event in the life of a fishing village. Annan and Stieglitz began to correspond in June 1895 when Stieglitz

FIG. 7
A Dutch Dog-cart *1892 in its frame*
Platinum
The frame may be to the design of George Walton.
Private Collection

wrote to ask if he would judge his 'Champion Competition' and they continued writing from time to time until 1942. Each had great admiration for the other's work.

¶ Annan appeared in London in October 1893 at the first Salon of the Linked Ring where *The Studio* hailed 'a consummate artist whose individuality is surprising.'[26] He sold two radically different works: *A Utrecht Pastoral*, a conventional landscape with echoes of Hobbema and *Fishers' Wives*, a startlingly minimal print, when its shapes are considered in the abstract.

¶ The Linked Ring had been formed in 1892 by dissidents from the Photographic Society of Great Britain. It wished to bring together those 'interested in the development of the highest form of Art of which Photography is capable.'[27] Despite its Gilbert and Sullivanish approach – its members had pseudonyms like H. P. Robinson's 'High Executioner' – it was a potent international force. Annan was elected on 6 February 1894, taking the name 'Selector'. He played a leading role as Centre Link, a sort of chairman, in the latter parts of 1896 and 1900. He wrote a paper for the other Links, about framing and exhibition design, which, as custom decreed, was printed in 'Olde Englishe'[28].

¶ In the astounding year of 1894 Annan could be forgiven a little pride. He leapt into the international limelight. In January he showed fifteen prints (more than anyone else) in the first exhibition of the *Photo-Club de Paris*. *Les Reflets* (*Reflections, Amsterdam*) was particularly admired. In April he exhibited at the Joint Exhibition in New York, including *Reflections, Amsterdam* and *The Beach at Zandvoort*. The latter, 'one of the gems of the exhibition', was used as the frontispiece to the magazine *The*

FIG. 8
Venice from the Lido
by D. Y. Cameron
Etching
No.17 of the 26 prints of the
North Italian Set *published by*
W. B. Paterson, Glasgow, 1896.
Glasgow Art Gallery and
Museum

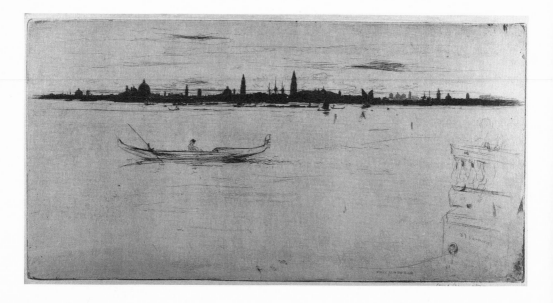

American Amateur Photographer that month. Its editor, Alfred Stieglitz, welcomed 'the first opportunity Americans have had to enjoy this artist's work. May we see more of it, for it is a good teacher.' Some time that year Annan's work was shown in Russia at the *IV Fotograficheskaya Vyvstavka* (4th Photographic Exhibition). His medal bears the inscription ИРТО. In October, at the second London Salon, he sold *The Lombardy Ploughing Team* (plate 11), one of the fruits of another expedition with Cameron.

¶ *Lombardy Pastoral* (plate 12) and *Ploughing on the Campagnetta* (plate 10) are of people and animals in the landscape. The former print is 4.7 × 14 cm and the latter 4.8 × 14.8 cm, tiny but powerful works. These are Annan's personal explorations of the current Realist movement which involved an interest in working life seen honestly. The photograph of ploughing was so effectively natural that Annan was forced to explain that it was indeed calculated: 'The teams of oxen *happened* to occupy the fortunate positions they do in the picture, but it was only after watching them plough furrow after furrow that I *chanced* to make the exposure.'[29] His 'instantaneous snapshot' was informed by a visual understanding of the ploughing which enabled him to capture its process.

¶ As Annan and Cameron travelled between Genoa and Venice each dealt with his own interests, but in Venice they decided to tackle the same view, *Venice from the Lido*. Each artist clearly expressed the aesthetic of his technique. Annan, having composed the posts in the water against the far towers, then needed to be patient until the idle oar of the gondola cut the skyline of the city exactly as he wished it to balance this sparse, abstract composition (plate 6). Cameron's etching needle had to be swift to record the drifting gondola and the movements of his needle are plain to see (fig. 8). Cameron was responding to the challenge of the snapshot camera, which may be seen on another occasion when he and Annan both captured the white friars. Annan took the instantaneous photograph of them striding forward (plate 5); Cameron, seconds later, etched them retreating (fig. 9).

¶ Annan's photogravures and Cameron's etchings were the result of a working friendship. Their influence on each other is the more interesting because their work is distinctive. Photogravure and etching share a common process in engraving and it is likely that it is here that their discussions were also intense.

¶ Annan would have known Whistler's Venice etchings, including those of the Riva, but the dreamy twilight in Annan's *Riva Schiavoni* (plate 7) is more like a Whistler painting. Annan left only one area in the print sharp, the upraised hand of the statue of Victor Emmanuel. The print was a particular favourite of his. Annan must have moved to the *Giudecca* to catch the *Franciscan of Il Redentore* (fig. 10) for the title of the print sug-

FIG. 9
Two Monks *1894*
by D. Y. Cameron
Etching
Glasgow Art Gallery and Museum

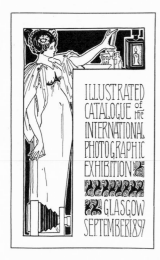

gests that the monk is associated with the fine church by Palladio. There is no clue where he ambushed *The White Friars* (plate 5) because the background of this print was faded out in case it detracted from the vigorous stride of the two monks. Even with advances in the speeds of films and shutters, this dynamic work still attracts attention for its sense of movement. In 1896 Annan published a folio, *Venice and Lombardy*, in a limited edition of seventy-five, each containing eleven original photogravures. Here are photographs treated as precious fine art objects.

¶ Annan wrote about his experiences with the new hand camera, which discarded the tripod, in *The Amateur Photographer* in 1896. Many people read his advice to the 'camerist', including Stieglitz, who mined it heavily for one of his own in *The American Annual of Photography* for 1897. Annan's article was translated for the bulletin of the *Photo-Club de Paris* in 1896, and in 1897 an extract from that was published in the bulletin of *L'Association Belge de Photographie*. Both Annan and Stieglitz in their articles agreed that the key was to set up the composition and then wait. Annan explained that to capture the *Franciscan* he had waited 'fully half an hour with the whole composition arranged and without making an exposure, before the old gentleman in brown habit came along, and he is unaware of the great service he did me.'[30] Stieglitz explained that his now famous photograph, *Winter – Fifth Avenue*, had been 'the result of a three hours' stand during a fierce snow-storm, awaiting the proper moment.'[31] Photography was taking an important step forward.

§ PHOTOGRAVURE

Although the International Photographic Exhibition in Glasgow in 1897 attracted photographers from as far as Russia and India, none was sufficiently outstanding to compete with Annan who swept the board with four of the six gold medals.

¶ The exhibition catalogue (fig. 11) gives a useful description of photogravure: 'Photogravure is an intaglio process, until recently shrouded in secrecy, the most beautiful of all photomechanical processes. In the process a copperplate well polished is dusted over with fine powdered bitumen or resin, and is heated sufficiently to melt the bitumen. Upon the plate so prepared a negative carbon print is mounted and developed, then etched in a solution of perchloride of iron, the action of the mordant being stopped directly the copper plate under the blackest portions of the carbon image is discoloured. The carbon tissue is now cleaned off, and after burnishing the edges, the plate is ready for printing. The plate is then gently heated, and ink rubbed over it and into all its depressions, the superfluous ink is then removed, leaving the ink in the depressions only. Damp paper is laid on to the plate and impressions are taken by means of a copper-plate press. For specimen of this process, see inset by Messrs. T. & R. Annan and Sons, Glasgow, from a Portrait of the Hon. Mrs Graham, painted by Gainsborough.'[32] The great appeal of photogravure is its ability to reproduce a wide range of tones in a permanent print. Because this process allows manipulation of the photographic image at its various stages by hand it offers opportunities for creative working. Finally, the artist can pull prints from the plate, or they can be produced mechanically in quantity. There is nothing 'instamatic' about photogravure for it demands great skill.[33]

¶ Annan used his consummate skill to manipulate his images to a greater degree than the observer at first realises. What seems a straightforward photograph is the product of considerable work after the exposure. Here lies a dichotomy. For example, Annan's print of the two striding monks, is, for all its spontaneity, the product of much labour on the plate, fading out the background and softening the forms. The blurring, which conveys the idea of motion, is not entirely the product of the lens. A second example is unexplained. The version of the *Franciscan of Il Redentore* (fig. 10) with lettering proves to be printed from a split negative. Close inspection of it reveals that Annan notched together two negatives.[34] The join is carefully hidden down the stones forming the end of the wall. Why this was done to an image which he quoted as an example of a quick capture 'with the whole composition arranged' remains a mystery. Working on the plate was a part of the process which he thoroughly enjoyed. 'The making of the negative is the first stage. While this initial operation requires great promptitude of action, the subsequent manipulation may be prolonged into a long-drawn-out pleasure.'[35] Cameron designed Annan's bookplate displaying not his camera but his engraving tools, caliper, roulettes, burnishers and scrapers (fig. 12) above the motto '*Ars est Celare Artem*' ('The Art is in its Concealment').

¶ After the turn of the century Annan's plates received a great deal of work. In *The White House* (plate 26) only the canopy on the barge in front of the house boat remains sharp though there are some touches to strengthen the trees above the house. Annan must have enjoyed immensely working over the stones of *Harlech Castle* (plate 24). The surface of *Bolney Backwater* (plate 25) is almost entirely burnished and *The Thames at Hampton* is so worked over as to suggest that Annan may have been attempting to make it look like an oil painting.

FIG. 12
Bookplate *for J. Craig Annan*
1892
by D. Y. Cameron
Etching
T. & R. Annan & Sons Ltd.,
Glasgow

FIG. 13
A Photograph from Life *1892*
From the illustration in The
Studio *vol.3, 1894, p.16.*
National Library of Scotland,
Edinburgh

¶ Certain images received different treatments. There is a soft, dreamy *Riva Schiavoni* (plate 7) and a stormy one. The clouds in *Stirling Castle* (plate 22) vary considerably. These variations are different enough for the prints to be considered as separate works. They are not the equivalent of impressions taken at different states from a plate by the etcher. The size of images, and therefore plates, also varies. *Stirling Castle* in *Camera Work* measures 14.9 × 21.6 cm. It also exists at 19.5 × 28.6 cm.

¶ So skilful was Annan that he produced a few prints to look like etchings: *A Photograph from Life* (fig.13), and another, larger version, with the head, only, of an added figure. It provoked a discussion in *The Studio*: 'An objection is that the action of light in photography does not draw in lines and therefore we have no right to use methods which appear to be contrary to the spirit of the art.'[36] What look like the marks of an etching needle appear in *Two Ladies of Verona* (plate 14).

¶ In the taking of exposures Annan is modern, but in the making of prints he is not. An early argument, that the camera, merely a machine, could not produce a work of art, received an answer from some photographers who manipulated their images to ensure that the hand of the creator was apparent. The gumbichromate process used a great deal on the Continent allowed this – and aped oil paint. Annan's manipulation remained discreet, rarely working against photographic qualities, so much so that when in 1911 Pictorialism was analysed and divided into two camps[37] with Demachy, Eugene and Edward Steichen defined as painter-like, Annan was placed with Stieglitz and White as those with true photographic intentions.

FIG. 14
Mrs Anne Rigby *c.1890*
Photogravure
One of a set of 20 photogravures
from Hill and Adamson
calotypes. In the calotype she
faces to the left.
Scottish National Portrait
Gallery, Edinburgh

§ PORTRAITS AND COSTUME PIECES

Annan made a wide range of fine portraits throughout his entire career. His portraiture displays a palpable lineage, through Thomas Annan, to Hill and Adamson. The influence of Whistler is also occasionally apparent as it was on many of his contemporaries, both painters and photographers alike.

¶ His best known portrait, *Janet Burnet* (plate 8), which was seen in Berlin, Bradford, Brussels, Buffalo, Glasgow, London and New York, proved immensely popular although it is not appreciated to the same extent today. Cameron described it as 'a masterpiece and one of the finest things in photography.'[38] The critics saw it as a relation of Whistler's *Mother* (1872, Louvre) but it bears a closer kinship to Hill and Adamson's *Mrs Rigby* (fig.14), which Annan knew well because he made photogravure prints of it from their calotype negative, and kept one on his mantlepiece. He said of it, 'There is no sweeter presentment of old age.'[39] Janet Burnet was the aunt of the architect John James Burnet. She was photographed at 18 University Avenue, Glasgow, in the architect's drawing room, which had low windows, with the soft flat light immediately behind the camera.

¶ The lettering incorporated in *Janet Burnet* and in *Ellen Terry* was inspired by Holbein's miniatures. Clarence White used lettering in the same way in *Letitia Felix* in 1901. *Robert Meldrum* (plate 9) has his name inscribed in a panel at the foot of his portrait, a device again from Holbein. The idea is taken further to make a bookplate from the portrait of Dorothy Carleton Smyth by adding 'Ex Libris'. In another version Annan continued with her name, using a letter form similar to that in the Holbein drawing, *The Lady Richmond*, at Windsor.

¶ One of his finest portraits is *The Etching Printer – William Strang Esq., A.R.A.* of 1902 (plate 13). Annan worked this plate agressively, fading out both background and foreground to allow concentration on the real subject which is an artist in the heat of work. Strang's darting glance assesses the etching plate resting so delicately on his fingers. This print is the product of Annan's manipulative skills and is done with immense panache. The extent of his manipulation can be judged by comparing a straight print from the negative (fig. 15). Even its proportions are slightly altered.[40]

¶ Annan photographed some of the 'Glasgow Boys' for *The Glasgow School of Painters*, published in 1908.[41] W. Y. Macgregor wrote of his portrait, 'It is like me when I go to town, and, as I told Annan, a brushed up toff will be some variety among such a lot of rugged geniuses.'[42] The title page announces '74 reproductions and portraits in photogravure by J. Craig Annan'.

FIG. 15
The Etching Printer – William Strang Esq., A. R. A. *1902*
Photograph, process unknown
Art Workers Guild, London

FIG. 16
C. R. Mackintosh *1893*
Modern print
Glasgow School of Art

It was a labour of love by someone who delighted in fine bookmaking, and among the fifty-four works of art reproduced was one belonging to Annan himself, Macaulay Stevenson's *Springtime*. In November Annan despatched a presentation copy to Stieglitz by way of an exchange for copies of his quarterly *Camera Work*.

¶ Annan caught the flair displayed by that group of strong women associated with the Glasgow School of Art. The book illustrator Jessie M. King (plate 15) also appears in two of only four known autochromes. She sits next to a shining bowl which resembles the quasi-mystical vessels found in the work of some Americans, Steichen's *The Brass Bowl* or Annie W. Brigman's *The Wondrous Globe*. The gifted teacher Anne Macbeth (plate 19), girt with a Glasgow-style collar embroidered with hearts and roses, leans forward, in a highly informal pose, suggesting something of the intensity of her character. She designed Suffragette banners which her students stitched.

¶ Annan created what has become the icon of the architect and designer C. R. Mackintosh (fig. 16) when he photographed him wearing his loose tie, and showing a minute kiss-curl on his forehead. Margaret Macdonald Mackintosh (plate 17) sits in their flat at 120 Mains Street, at the beginning of the new century and her marriage to Mackintosh. Annan chose to show, behind her, the desk her husband designed with panels which she probably made, a happy statement on their relationship. He positioned the camera unusually low, about waist level, to enhance her presence. Anna Muthesius (plate 18) (then persistently spelt Mathasius), one of the Mackintoshes's friends, is also taken with a low camera. Her standing collar sweeps the eye up to her feathered hat in a *fin de siècle* fashion plate. She was once a professional singer, now wife of the German cultural attaché Hermann Muthesius. He championed Mackintosh's work. She wrote about dress and embroidery. Fra Newbery, Director of the Glasgow School of Art, and also a photographer, painted her embroidering in 1904. The wife of Annan's friend Cameron is also shown embroidering, wearing a dress which displays her skills on its armlets and collar (plate 20). The vase with a branch of blossom hints at *Japonisme*.

¶ Of his contemporaries involved in photography he took Juhl in 1893, F. Holland Day in 1901 (who returned the compliment),[43] and Alvin Langdon Coburn about 1906. Annan knew George Bernard Shaw as both practitioner and defender of photography. His portrait was taken in 1910, Shaw examining a picture by Muirhead Bone. Annan captured several literary figures. S. R. Crockett's portrait is inscribed with his name and the date, 1895, the year this Free Church minister gave up his charge to become a best selling *Kailyard* author. The portrait was taken in Crockett's own room, the background a rug thrown over a screen. Hilaire Belloc was photographed in 1910. The composition of *G. K. Chesterton* (plate 16), in 1912, head, hands and spectacles, is surely stylistically descended from Hill and Adamson. Compare their composition of head, hands and book in *Professor Alexander Monro* (fig. 17) of which Annan had made a photogravure. He photographed Joseph Conrad in his Glasgow hotel bedroom in 1923.

¶ To produce what could be classified as costume pieces Annan sometimes used members of the local dramatic society. Was there a Shakespeare production in Lenzie in 1897 to prompt *Two Ladies of Verona*? Perhaps it is the least successful area in an extremely wide breadth of practice. One of the earliest and most unfortunate is *The Church or the World* of 1893 with its allegorical pretensions. The title often appeared as *The Church and the World*, completely changing its meaning. The image was printed sometimes with the pony facing right, and sometimes left, as if the rider were undecided on the way ahead. *Camera Notes* called it 'the sheerest travesty'.[44]. Nevertheless, Stieglitz collected it and Demachy adored it. *The Painter's Page* was a boy employed 'in the studios of two of our foremost painters'[45] but neither a print nor an illustration of it has surfaced. *The Little Princess* was Muriel Wylie Hill posing for Walton's brother, Edward. In 1895 the painting appeared in *Fair Children* at the Grafton Gallery and the photograph at the Salon. Next year, at the *Photo-Club de Paris* visitors stood *'ravis, devant "La Petite Princesse"'*.[46] They invoked Van Dyck. It was Velázquez the Belgians invoked when they saw her in Brussels in 1897.

¶ *Eleänore* (fig. 18) is accompanied by four lines from Tennyson:

> *As tho' a star in inmost heaven set*
> *So full, so deep, so slow,*
> *Thought seems to come and go*
> *In thy large eyes, imperial Eleänore.*[47]

At the Salon in 1896 she was priced at £5.10/-, higher than usual, but then Annan was attempting to photograph unreality. The steep slope in the background prepares the viewer for the idea that Eleänore was born 'a mile beneath the cedar-wood'. She roamed, as Annan shows, 'with tresses unconfined . . . between the sunset and the moon'. When she utters the poet's name he will die, but that is what he desires. The closing lines (not quoted by Annan) make a fine climax for Post-Freudians:

> *Yet tell my name again to me,*
> *I would be dying evermore,*
> *So dying ever, Eleänore.*

FIG. 17
Professor Alexander Monro
c.1890
Photogravure
One of a set of 20 photogravures
from Hill and Adamson
calotypes.
Scottish National Portrait
Gallery, Edinburgh

FIG. 18
Eleänore *1896*
Photogravure
From Die Kunst in der
Photographie *vol.4, no.5, 1900.*
National Museum of
Photography, Film and
Television, Bradford. By
courtesy of the Board of
Trustees of the Science Museum

§ EXHIBITIONS

The decade was crowned for Annan in February 1900 by a one man show, the first presented by the Royal Photographic Society, despite his membership of the Linked Ring. He noted: 'I valued the honour as I had been in the opposition camp.'[48] His celebrity was such that when he arrived in London to hang the exhibition, *The Amateur Photographer* surprised him, near midnight, at Euston station and was supplied with a copy of his opening speech.[49] He said:

¶ 'If a picture has any real merit, it should touch a sympathetic chord in the intelligence of the observer, and give him pleasure. If it does so, it has fulfilled its mission, but if it does not, no amount of argument will enable him to realise and enjoy the artistic intention of the producer. The aim of a picture is not to demonstrate any theory or fact, but is to excite a certain sensory pleasure. Study the work of the great art masters. It is not sufficient that we should make a point of visiting picture galleries, or that we should provide ourselves with a collection of reproductions which we store in a cupboard. We must have them upon our walls, that we may absorb their influence as unconsciously as the air we breath. We must surround ourselves with the most beautiful objects which we can procure, and, what is equally important, we must exclude everything from our immediate surroundings which is antagonistic to beauty. By accustoming one's self constantly to see things of beauty, one becomes more sensitive and more able to discriminate rapidly and it is this power of rapid discrimination which is the most useful attribute a photographer can possess.'

¶ Annan took this seriously for he had Walton design the interior of the family home in 1897. Glimpses of it are seen in the backgrounds of some of his portraits (fig. 19). His extreme care extended to framing, then a vexed subject. Of broad wooden frames he said: 'I have never been able to rest content with such frames which decorate my own rooms. In preparing this collection I have framed my photographs in mounts of a light cream or straw colour. I have endeavoured to obviate the suddenness of the impact of the light mount upon the picture by a series of lines, either in delicate ink or in dull ruling, drawn round the opening of the mount.' Antwerp Museum of Photography holds *Sibylla*, the print shown at the *Photo-Club de Paris* in 1896 in its broad gallery frame. Its corners are not dovetailed but the uprights are inserted into the horizontals to afford a decorative touch, perhaps to a design by Walton. Annan had another highly artistic solution. The frame of *Molly* (fig. 20) was commissioned in 1897 from Frances and Margaret Macdonald who beat it out of aluminium in high Glasgow style. From a heart-shaped seed, daisies grow up either side of the frame to be met at the top by a row of butterflies, altogether happier than their more usual angst-ridden designs. Annan sold *Molly* for 10 guineas but the frame had cost him half that sum.

¶ Annan hung his pictures at the Royal Photographic Society in a tight band along the top of the dado and up and over the fireplace. It was an extreme arrangement, but part of an experiment to re-consider the presentation of photographic exhibitions. In this the Linked Ring led the way. Annan believed, as did Mackintosh, in total design. The scheme for the Linked Ring Salon in 1897 probably came about by Annan introducing his friend Walton, barely arrived in London, to the Ring. *The Photogram* described Walton's treatment of the gallery: 'At the top of the walls a broad green valance. Next to this a frieze of buff canvas or sackcloth, neither festooned nor tightly stretched, and here and there a conventional – or should we say unconventional – pattern stencilled. Next a continuous shelf in white wood placed just to avoid cutting the wall equally into two portions. The pictures are hung irregularly, but in this plan resides the designer's cunning. The intervals between the frames vary from half-an-inch to as much as nine or twelve inches, and a little design of lotus, lily, or leaf is drawn on the canvas background.'[50] A less convinced review commented: 'Pictures higgledy-piggledy – in other words, obedient to the glorious gospel of haphazard, most carefully pre-arranged. The little designs in pastel on the wall surface, even the frames, are puerile. The hanging is not free from affectation. But there is one very real value. In a scheme where the frames are in horizontal bands the eye slides along the line. By the present plan, each picture arrests your attention, and for this reason the Salon deserves praise.'[51]

¶ Walton received several commissions from his photographic connections. These led to a whiff of Glasgow style in Berlin, Brussels, Dublin, Glasgow, London, Milan, Moscow, St Petersburg and Vienna, from the Kodak showrooms he designed between 1898 and 1903.

¶ The Glasgow International Exhibition of 1901 celebrated the opening of the city's Art Gallery. Into this new gallery went the new art of photography, 'works of artistic value from nature [which] owe their various qualities to the individual sentiment of their producers.'[52] Annan was Convenor of the photography committee and the exhibition was very much his own. In July 1900 he visited Berlin, Brussels, Dresden, Hamburg, Munich, Paris and Vienna, and he scrutinised the Royal Photographic Society exhibition and the Salon. He contacted Alexis Mazourine for Russian contributions. He wrote, as a Fellow Link, to Stieglitz for help with the American section. With few exceptions Stieglitz's selection formed the exhibition in 1902

FIG. 20
Frame *for 'Molly' 1897
by Margaret Macdonald and
Frances Macdonald
Beaten aluminium on wood
From* The Photogram *vol.5,
1895, p.58.
Glasgow School of Art*

[25

which Stieglitz announced as the work of The Photo-Secession. Glasgow had a preview of an important moment in American photography.

¶ Annan hung each country in a bay, on dark green-brown walls. The two hundred and one exhibitors consisted of groups from America, England, France (the *Photo Club de Paris*) and Scotland, and smaller representations from Austria, Belgium, Germany, India, Italy, Russia and Switzerland. Was there another pictorial photography exhibition with this geographic spread? The old debate that a photograph could not carry the personal imprint of its creator moved on during that summer. The game was to spot national characteristics. *The British Journal of Photography* was certain: 'The French beautiful and chic, the German massive and strong, the American intellectual and poetic.'[53] This might have been a topic grappled by 'The Glasgow International Assembly', run by Professor Patrick Geddes, when they met in the photographic galleries. Visitors saw now familiar pictorial works including: Day's *Ebony and Ivory*; Frederick Evans's *Wells Cathedral*; Theodor and Oskar Hofmeister's *After Sundown*; Gertrude Käsebier's *The Manger*; Constant Puyo's *Chant Sacré*; Stieglitz's *Winter, Fifth Avenue*; and White's *Ring Toss*. Frank Sutcliffe's *The Water Rats* seemed 'to speak of a bygone age in its mottled mount and gilt frame.'[54] There was also a photograph which had acted as a catalyst to new thinking, George Davison's *The Onion Field*. Annan exhibited *Janet Burnet* (plate 8), *Summer*, a portrait of Professor John Young and one of W. Q. Orchardson. Ironically, a photographic record of this exhibition remains to be found. Most of the eleven and a half million visitors to the exhibition saw the photographs, which were hung in Gallery One.

¶ It was a tribute to Annan's influence and standing in the world of art that photography was invited to take such a prominent position. Stieglitz writing in *Camera Notes* was amazed: 'Glasgow offered no prizes of any kind. The invitation to exhibit on equal footing with painters, sculptors, architects was the sole honor sought by those loving their art. It was the first time in the history of Pictorial Photography that it found itself welcomed and officially recognised in the cathedral of Fine Art simultaneously with its older sisters.'[55] This was not the case three years later when at the St Louis Exposition, where Annan was a jury member, photography was refused a home with the Arts and was placed with Industry.

¶ The Glasgow International Exhibition of 1901 proved a triumph for Annan and a financial success for his firm, the official photographers. As a result they could afford a handsome new home at 518 Sauchiehall Street (fig. 21) designed in 1903 by John Keppie of Honeyman, Keppie and Mackintosh.

§ LATER WORK

There is a profound development in Annan's art after the turn of the century. His landscapes, though not the products of trips to foreign countries as before, were all taken away from home. His now large photogravures were printed from heavily worked plates. Their titles refer only obliquely to the subject of the prints. While the sources which inspired his earlier work are patent, Annan had found, within himself, a well of pure water. His work became sombre, introspective, imbued with a quite extraordinary mood which he conjured out of the most ordinary subject matter.

¶ This mood is heralded in *The Dark Mountains* of 1890, photographed on Ben Vorlich (plate 21). It appeared at the Linked Ring Salon in 1895, then in Philadelphia, Dresden, and at the Royal Photographic Society. It was reproduced in *Photographisches Centralblatt* in 1899, in *The Amateur Photographer* in 1903 and in *Camera Work* in 1904. In 1895 it was perceived as an Old Testament subject – 'Moses is certainly suggested'.[56] In 1901 another critic read into it 'Walpurgian nightmares or Dantesque dreams, ideas of massive, awful grandeur, unknown threatening dangers.'[57] By 1986 it had become a 'Romantic landscape in the tradition of Caspar David Friedrich.'[58] It was the earliest dated print bought by Stieglitz. Juhl had a copy which he lent to the exhibition in Dresden. Matthies-Masuren owned a brown carbon print made through linen, now in Berlin. How did Annan render so intriguing four men on a mountain ridge? They walk away, presenting their backs to the viewer who thus becomes one of their group. There is an invitation to follow them to the glow far ahead, across the ranges, under the lowering sky. He evokes half-forgotten ideas of quest or pilgrimage.

¶ *Stirling Castle* of 1906 is a superb example of Annan's skill in photogravure (plate 22). Its range of tones 'from silver to velvet' was noted by *Photograms of the Year* in 1906 when it hung in the Salon. It was reproduced in *Camera Work* in July 1907. The photograph clearly stems from an outing with William Strang, or from his etching *The Farm Yard*, dated 1895. Strang stood further to the right, for he depicts the entire round building which was a horse mill. The photogravure is no commercial tourist view of Stirling Castle as produced by Washington Wilson or Valentine. The castle appears grandly romantic atop its volcanic crag, but it merely oversees the farmyard beneath.[59] Annan is interested in the roofs of the farm building, the way the tiles come round the circular roof on the work-mill, the way the tiles fit together, the pattern they make. A white horse stands alone in the yard. It seems to echo the white clouds in the sky. Perhaps it has just landed from one of them.[60] His friend Cameron, with a special insight, described his photography as 'reticent, reserved, weird, and tenderly beautiful'.[61] These are the qualities of *Stirling Castle*. It is difficult to explain the impact of this powerful work made from the most unexceptional and momentary happenings. Annan had strong views about explaining art (see page 24): that it should strike 'a sympathetic chord and give pleasure ... but if it does not, no amount of argument will enable him to realise and enjoy the artistic intention of the producer.'[62] The difficulty in explaining does not undermine the aesthetic pleasure of his gravure.

¶ In 1907 Annan was four miles south-west of Clitheroe in Lancashire to photograph *Stonyhurst*, a fine Elizabethan building with added Baroque cupolas at its gatehouse (plate 23). Annan liked to work over the walls of such buildings. The light in this print is to a large degree the product of Annan's handiwork on the plate, though it is just possible that the shadows were being cast at forty-five degrees when he made the exposure. The empty grounds add to the tension of the threatening weather.

¶ Bolney is about ten miles south of Crawley in East Sussex, but *Bolney Backwater* (plate 25) of 1908 is not in the least specific. What activity prompted Annan to release his shutter, at that precise moment?

¶ Annan visited George Davison in January 1909 when he photographed *Harlech Castle* (plate 24). Davison produced a *Harlech Castle* which was printed by Annan for *Camera Work* in April 1909. He showed the castle in the landscape but Annan preferred a detail with few clues to the building's identity. Snow has outlined its steps and wall. The air is cold and quiet. The icy light is fading. There seems to be no tangible activity to prompt the exposure. The faintest of echoes inhabit this uncanny print.

¶ Davison, recently retired from the post of Managing Director of Kodak in Britain, had Walton build *The White House*, 'an art nouveau version of the Regency style',[63] at Shiplake, four miles upstream from Henley-on-Thames. Annan joined Davison in July 1909 when it was just completed. In front of it was moored Davison's houseboat *The Log Cabin*,[64] also designed by Walton. Annan's *The White House* (plate 26) is redolent of shimmering summer, indolence and wealth. It is quintessential Annan: the view carefully set up, but the exposure not made until the punt (in which Davison's son Ronald sits) has drifted into the exact position to complete the composition.

¶ When the Ring unlinked in 1910 Annan was among those who formed the London Secession. It held only one exhibition. He exhibited at the Kodak Gallery in Liverpool in 1912 and at *The Amateur Photographer*'s premises in London in 1913, but gradually his exhibiting activities ceased.

¶ In 1913 he went to Spain with William Strang. Similar subjects attracted him as before. He caught the delicate movement of two animals as they moved a heavily laden cart in *Bullock Cart, Burgos* (plate 28). However, there is one difference. This time people posed: *A Gitana (Gipsy) Returning from Market* (plate 27) against a white wall, or paused, in *Group on a Hill Road, Granada* (plate 29). He never found time to produce an album of Spanish subjects, but Stieglitz published eight in *Camera Work* in January 1914.

¶ Annan missed acutely the excitements in Glasgow at the turn of the century and his interest shifted. By 1919 he was dealing in etchings. He wrote to Stieglitz: 'Last week I sold a Rembrandt etching *Selfportrait leaning on a stone sill*. It is one of his masterpieces. Many Dürer engravings and etchings of Whistler have come to Glasgow so my life is as full of interest as ever.'[65] There may have been a sound commercial reason for this change; not much photogravure was being produced by the firm. Annan faded from the photography scene. Stieglitz wrote to Heinrich Kuehn on 15 August 1923: 'I haven't heard anything of Annan for four years. He has his reproduction business in Glasgow – and also a gallery where he exhibits and sells etchings. He no longer exhibits his photographs because there are no first class photography exhibitions any more. Annan is a fine person.'[66]

¶ Annan was an influential, international figure. As a practising photographer, his views that photography could be a fine art were eagerly read in photographic journals, while his magnificent prints, often in the beautiful process of photogravure, demonstrated the fact in exhibitions throughout Europe and America. He preached the importance of design and framing. His photography, highly accomplished technically, is always fastidious. It was at first, fresh, vital, and forward-looking, then, latterly, mellow and introspective. He was an adventurous artist, respecting the photographic image but never over-awed by it when he saw an opportunity to be creative. In the manipulation of his images he was a man of his times, but as 'a connoisseur of transience'[67] he clearly signalled a way ahead. He was in Stieglitz's words: 'A true artist, and a decidedly poetic one at that.'[68] His *The White House* is now seen, with Stieglitz's *Going to the Start* and Paul Haviland's *Passing Steamer*, as one of the 'seminal examples of the instantaneous snapshot wedded to the formal concerns of modern art.'[69]

¶ 'James Craig Annan, Photographer and Fine Art Dealer (Retired) (Single)'[70] died on 5 June 1946. The etchings he bequeathed to Glasgow Art Gallery included Rembrandt's *Faust* (fig. 22). This shows an alchemist studying a magic disc through which light pours. So must Annan have carefully studied his magic disc, the lens of his camera.

FIG. 22
Faust *c.1652*
by Rembrandt van Rijn
Etching
Glasgow Art Gallery and
Museum

NOTES

AP *The Amateur Photographer*
CN *Camera Notes*
CW *Camera Work*
PY *Photograms of the Year*

1 PY, 1895, p.84.

2 PY, 1898, p.33.

3 PY, 1900, p.14.

4 Joseph Keily, 'The Philadelphia Salon', CN, vol.2, no.3, January 1899, p.119.

5 A. C. R. Carter, 'The Photographic Salon', PY, 1901, p.98.

6 Snowden Ward, 'Some Notes on Pictorial Photography', PY, 1909, p.10.

7 Joseph Keily, 'The Salon', CN, vol.3, no.3, January 1900, p.151.

8 Frederick Evans, 'The Photographic Salon', AP, 21 September 1909, p.294.

9 Dudley Johnstone, 'Obituary James Craig Annan, Honorary Fellow', *The Photographic Journal*, July 1946, p.174.

10 Joseph Keily, 'Loan Exhibition', CN, vol.3, no.4, April 1900, p.214.

11 Joseph Keily, 'The Salon', CN, vol.4, no.3, January 1901, p.98.

12 'Men You Know', *The Bailie*, 31 August 1904, p.1.

13 Helmut Gernsheim, *A Concise History of Photography*, New York 1986 (3rd revised edition), p.61.

14 Now in the Glasgow School of Art Library.

15 *The British Journal of Photography*, 19 April 1878, p.185.

16 Quoted by permission of T. & R. Annan & Sons Ltd., Glasgow.

17 Letter, 27 February 1883, in the possession of T. & R. Annan & Sons Ltd., Glasgow.

18 Matthew Surface, 'Our Leaders', *The Practical Photographer*, 8 June 1896, p.154-157.

19 Unattributed, 'Men You Know', *The Bailie*, 31 August 1904.

20 Unattributed, 'Studio Talk', *The Scots Pictorial*, vol.5, no.85, 12 November 1898, p.250.

21 'Mr Craig Annan's Address at the Opening of the Exhibition of his Works at the Royal Photographic Society', AP, 2 February 1900, p.83.

22 J. Craig Annan, 'Picture-Making with the Hand-Camera; or, the use of the Hand-camera for Pictorial results', AP, 27 March 1896, p.275.

23 W. J. Warren, 'J. Craig Annan', AP, 29 September 1899, p.251.

24 *The Practical Photographer*, no.13, 1904, reproduced in green 'Fishers' Wives', opp. p.8 and 'Reflections', opp. p.16.

25 Weston Naef, *The Collection of Alfred Stieglitz*, New York, 1978.

26 Theodore Wratislaw, 'The Photographic Salon', *The Studio*, vol.2, 1894, p.68.

27 Margaret Harker, *The Linked Ring*, London 1979, p.ix.

28 'Selector', untitled, *Linked Ring Papers*, no.6, 10 November 1896, unpaginated.

29 J. Craig Annan, *op. cit.*, note 21, p.83.

30 *ibid*.

31 Alfred Stieglitz, 'The Hand Camera', *The American Annual of Photography for 1897*, p.19.

32 David C. Coghill, 'Photo-mechanical Printing', Catalogue of the International Exhibition of Photography, Glasgow 1897.

33 See Johan de Zoete, *A Manual of Photogravure*, Haarlem 1988.

34 I am grateful to James Berry for pointing this out.

35 J. Craig Annan, *op. cit.*, note 22, p.275.

36 'A. M.' (Alfred Maskell), 'On some Methods of Suppression and Modification in Pictorial Photography', *The Studio*, vol.3, 1894, p.13.

37 Sadakichi Hartmann, 'What Remains', CW, 33, January 1911, p.30.

38 D. Y. Cameron, 'An Artist's Notes on Mr J. Craig Annan's Pictures now being Exhibited at the Royal Photographic Society', AP, 16 February 1900, p.123.

39 J. Craig Annan, 'David Octavius Hill RSA – 1802–1870', CW, 11 July 1905, p.17.

40 This is the only known surviving example of both a print and a manipulated photogravure from the same image. I am grateful to Sara Stevenson for sharing her discovery with me.

41 G. Baldwin Brown, *The Glasgow School of Painters*, Glasgow 1908.

42 Letter to James Paterson quoted in William Buchanan (ed.), *The Glasgow Boys*, Part Two. Exhibition Catalogue, The Scottish Arts Council, p.5.

43 Illustrated, PY, 1901, p.13.

44 Joseph Keily, 'The Salon', CN, vol.3, no.3, January 1900, p.151.

45 Unattributed, 'The Photographic Salon', PY, 1897, p.98.

46 *Bulletin du Photo-Club de Paris*, 1896, p.235.

47 Robert Stange (ed.), *The Poetical Works of Tennyson*, Boston 1974, 'Eleänore', p.22.

48 Annan, typescript, 1946 in the collection of T. & R. Annan & Sons Ltd., Glasgow.

49 J. Craig Annan, *op. cit.* note 21, p.83.

50 A. Horsley Hinton, *The Photogram*, November 1897, p.317.

51 Unattributed, 'The Photographic Salon', PY, 1897, p.93.

52 Official Report, 25 September 1901.

53 *The British Journal of Photography*, 3 May 1901, p.280.

54 Unattributed, 'Photograms at the Glasgow Exhibition', PY, 1901, p.13.

55 Alfred Stieglitz, 'Irreconcilable Positions – A Letter and the Reply', CN, January 1902, p.217.

56 Unattributed, 'The Two Great Exhibitions', PY, 1895, p.42.

57 Joseph Keily, 'The Salon', CN, vol.4, no.3, January 1901, p.198.

58 Mike Weaver, *The Photographic Art*, Exhibition Catalogue, The Scottish Arts Council, 1986, p.64.

59 This farm, Craigforth, is now covered by a fire station at the end of Craigforth Crescent where it meets Raploch Road.

60 William Buchanan, 'The "most versatile and artistic" James Craig Annan', *The Photographic Collector*, vol.5, no.1, 1984.

61 D. Y. Cameron, *op. cit.*, note 38, p.123.

62 J. Craig Annan, *op. cit.*, note 21, p.83.

63 Sherwood & Pevsner, *Oxfordshire*, London 1974, p.405.

64 Steichen's autochrome, 'On the House-boat – "The Log Cabin"' is illustrated in CW, April 1908, p.9.

65 Letter, 6 September 1919. Quoted by permission of Yale University, Collection of American Literature, the Beinecke Rare Book and Manuscript Library.

66 Unattributed, 'Letters to Henrich Kuehn', *Camera*, June, no.6, 1977, p.36.

67 Ian Jeffrey, *Photography: a Concise History*, Thames & Hudson, 1981, p.98.

68 Alfred Stieglitz, 'The Seventh Joint Annual Exhibition', *American Amateur Photographer*, 6 May 1894, p.209.

69 Jonathan Green, *Camera Work: A Critical Anthology*, Aperture, 1973, p.22.

70 Death Certificate, Registrar General.

PLATES

I LADY IN BLACK DRESS c.1890
Photogravure 21.5 × 15.8
One of a set of twenty photogravures made from Hill and
Adamson calotypes
Scottish National Portrait Gallery, Edinburgh

2   THE BEACH AT ZANDVOORT 1892
  Photogravure 4.6 × 23.3 (reproduced actual size)
  The Metropolitan Museum of Art, New York
  (The Alfred Stieglitz Collection)

3 ON A DUTCH SHORE 1892
Also known as A Fish Auction, Zandvoort
Photogravure 15.3 × 23.4
T. & R. Annan & Sons Ltd., Glasgow

4   THE ROAD THROUGH THE SAND DUNES 1892
    Photogravure 14.6 × 20.2
    From Die Kunst in der Photographie, *vol.4, no.5, 1900*
    National Museum of Photography, Film and Television,
    Bradford
    By courtesy of the Board of Trustees of the Science Museum

5   THE WHITE FRIARS 1894
Photogravure 10.1 × 9.3
No. 11 in the folio Venice and Lombardy
Scottish National Portrait Gallery, Edinburgh
(Riddell Collection)

6 VENICE FROM THE LIDO 1894
Photogravure 10 × 15
No. 1 in the folio Venice and Lombardy
Scottish National Portrait Gallery, Edinburgh
(Riddell Collection)

7   RIVA SCHIAVONI 1894
Photogravure 10.8 × 14.7
No. 6 in the folio Venice and Lombardy
Scottish National Portrait Gallery, Edinburgh
(Riddell Collection)

8 JANET BURNET 1893
Photogravure 20.4 × 16.8
Harker Farrand Collection

9   ROBERT MELDRUM 1898
Photogravure 20.8 × 9.3
T. & R. Annan & Sons Ltd., Glasgow

10   PLOUGHING ON THE CAMPAGNETTA 1894
Photogravure 5 × 15
No. 7 in the folio Venice and Lombardy
Scottish National Portrait Gallery, Edinburgh
(Riddell Collection)

12   LOMBARDY PASTORAL 1894
Photogravure 4.8 × 14.3
Scottish National Portrait Gallery, Edinburgh
(Riddell Collection)

11 LOMBARDY PLOUGHING TEAM 1894
Photogravure 11.1 × 27.7 (reproduced actual size)
Scottish National Portrait Gallery, Edinburgh
(Riddell Collection)

13   THE ETCHING PRINTER – WILLIAM STRANG ESQ.,
     A.R.A. 1902
     Photogravure 15.3 × 19.8
     From Annan's own copy of Camera Work, *no.19, July*
     1907, plate 2
     The Mitchell Library, Glasgow

14 TWO LADIES OF VERONA 1897
    Photogravure 21.6 × 28.7
    T. & R. Annan & Sons Ltd., Glasgow

15   JESSIE M. KING *c*.1906
      Platinum 20.6 × 15.6
      Scottish National Portrait Gallery, Edinburgh

16 G. K. CHESTERTON, ESQ. 1912
Carbon 20.7 × 15.8
National Portrait Gallery, London

17   MARGARET MACDONALD MACKINTOSH *c.*1901
Modern print
Private Collection

18 FRAU MUTHESIUS *c.*1900
Photogravure 21.9 × 15.8
T. & R. Annan & Sons Ltd., Glasgow

19   ANN MACBETH c.1908
Modern print
Private Collection

23 STONYHURST 1907
Photogravure 26.5 × 24.1
Scottish National Portrait Gallery, Edinburgh
(Riddell Collection)

22   STIRLING CASTLE 1906
Photogravure 19.5 × 28.5
Scottish National Portrait Gallery, Edinburgh

21 THE DARK MOUNTAINS 1890
Photogravure 15.1 × 20.4
T. & R. Annan & Sons Ltd., Glasgow

20   MRS D. Y. CAMERON *c.*1900
Modern print
T. & R. Annan & Sons Ltd., Glasgow

24 HARLECH CASTLE 1909
Photogravure 20.8 × 32.1
Scottish National Portrait Gallery, Edinburgh
(Riddell Collection)

25   BOLNEY BACKWATER 1908
Photogravure 21.7 × 28.5
Scottish National Portrait Gallery, Edinburgh
(Riddell Collection)

26   THE WHITE HOUSE 1909
Photogravure 25.7 × 24.2
Scottish National Portrait Gallery, Edinburgh
(Riddell Collection)

27   A GITANA (GYPSY) RETURNING FROM MARKET 1913
Also known as A Gitana, Granada
Photogravure 19.7 × 13.8
Scottish National Portrait Gallery, Edinburgh

28 BULLOCK CART, BURGOS 1913
Photogravure 14.6 × 17.3
T. & R. Annan & Sons Ltd., Glasgow

29   GROUP ON A HILL ROAD, GRANADA 1913
     Photogravure 11.3 × 18
     The Metropolitan Museum of Art, New York
     (The Alfred Stieglitz Collection)

COLLECTIONS
SELECT BIBLIOGRAPHY
BIOGRAPHIES

COLLECTIONS

Works by James Craig Annan are held in the following collections:

EUROPE

ANTWERP
Provinciaal Museum voor Fotografie

BATH
Royal Photographic Society

BERLIN
Staatliche Museen Preussischer Kulturbesitz, Kunstbibliothek

DRESDEN
Staatliche Kunstsammlungen, Kupferstich-Kabinett

EDINBURGH
Scottish Photography Archive, Scottish National Portrait Gallery

GLASGOW
T. & R. Annan & Sons Ltd.
School of Art Library
University Library

HAMBURG
Museum für Kunst und Gewerbe

LONDON
National Portrait Gallery
Victoria & Albert Museum

U.S.A.

AUSTIN
University of Texas

BUFFALO
Albright-Knox Art Gallery

CHICAGO
Art Institute

CLEVELAND
Museum of Art

MINNEAPOLIS
Institute of Arts

NEW YORK
Metropolitan Museum of Art
Museum of Modern Art

PHILADELPHIA
Museum of Art

ROCHESTER, NY
International Museum of Photography

WASHINGTON
National Museum of American History

SELECT BIBLIOGRAPHY

1978
Marianne Fulton Margolis (ed.)
Camera Work: A Pictorial Guide
Dover, New York
The reproductions do not approach the
quality of the originals

1978
Weston J. Naef
*The Collection of Alfred Stieglitz: Fifty
Pioneers of Modern Photography*
Metropolitan Museum/Viking, New York

1979
Margaret Harker
*The Linked Ring: The Secession Movement in
Photography in Britain, 1892–1910*
Royal Photographic Society/Heineman,
London

1980
Peter C. Bunnell (ed.)
*A Photographic Vision: Pictorial Photography,
1889–1923*
Peregrine Smith, Salt Lake City
A selection of key texts from European and
American sources

1981
Ian Jeffrey
Photography: A Concise History
Thames & Hudson, London

1983
William Innes Homer
Alfred Stieglitz and the Photo-Secession
Little, Brown and Company, Boston

1984
William Buchanan
'James Craig Annan: Brave Days in Glasgow'
Mark Haworth-Booth (ed.)
*The Golden Age of British Photography 1839–
1900*
Aperture/Victoria and Albert Museum

1984
Naomi Rosenblum
A World History of Photography
Abbeville Press, New York

1986
Erika and Fritz Kempe, Heinz Spielman
Die Kunst der Camera im Jugendstil:
Photographische Avantgarde von 1890 bis 1910
Umschau, Frankfurt

1989
William Buchanan
'J. Craig Annan and D. Y. Cameron in North
Holland'
Mike Weaver (ed.)
British Photography in the Nineteenth Century:
The Fine Art Tradition
Cambridge University Press

1990
Sara Stevenson
Thomas Annan 1829–1887
National Galleries of Scotland, Edinburgh

CATALOGUES

1978
John Taylor
Pictorial Photography in Britain 1900–1920
Arts Council of Great Britain/Royal
Photographic Society

1983
Margaret Harker, Pool Andries, Roger Coenen
La Photographie D'Art vers 1900
Crédit Communal, Bruxelles

1984
Janet E. Buerger
The Last Decade: The Emergence of Art
Photography in the 1890s
International Museum of Photography at
George Eastman House, Rochester, N.Y.

PERIODICALS

1897–1902
Alfred Stieglitz (ed.) *Camera Notes*
The Camera Club of New York

1897–1908
Franz Goerke (ed.)
Die Kunst in der Photographie Becker, Berlin,
(after 1900 other publishers)

1903–1917
Alfred Stieglitz (ed.)
Camera Work
Alfred Stieglitz, New York

1984–1985
Ulrich F. Keller
'The Myth of Art Photography'
Heinz K. Henisch (ed.)
History of Photography
vol.8, no.4, Oct.-Dec., Part 1, 'A Sociological
Analysis', p.249
vol.9, no.1, Jan.-Mar., Part 2, 'An
Iconographical Analysis', p.78
Taylor & Francis, London

BIOGRAPHIES

ANNIE W. BRIGMAN
1869–1950
Worked in the U.S.A. Member of the PS and the LR. Published in CW. 1902 exhibited at the second San Franciscan Photographic Salon. 1949 published *Songs of a Pagan*, a book of poems and photographs.

JULIA MARGARET CAMERON
1815–79
Worked in England and Ceylon. Her photographs taken mainly in the 1860s consisted of religious, literary and allegorical tableaux and portraiture. Her sitters included Herschel, Carlyle and Tennyson who commissioned a series of photographs to illustrate his *Idylls of the King*. Published, posthumously, in CW and inspired the Pictorialists.

ALVIN LANGDON COBURN
1882–1966
Worked in the U.S.A. and England. 1898 introduced to photography by a distant cousin F. Holland Day. 1902–03 worked in studio of Gertrude Käsebier. 1904 visited Annan and studied his photogravures of Hill and Adamson leading to an interest in that medium. Published in CW and in DKP. Member of the PS and the LR. 1906 decorated and hung the London Salon. Settled permanently in London. Published his photogravures in *London* 1909, *New York* 1910 and *Men of Mark* 1913, the latter including portraits of some of the Vorticists. 1917 made abstract Vortographs. 1930 donated his collection of photographs, which included seven Annans, to the Royal Photographic Society.

WILLIAM CROOKE
Worked in Scotland. 1883 opened an opulent portrait studio at 103 Princes Street, Edinburgh. Worked principally in sepia platinotype and brown carbon. 1892 exhibited at the *Exposition de l'Art Photographique Anglais* in Brussels and that year elected to the LR. Exhibited at the *Photo-Club de Paris*. Published in DKP. In July 1898 *The Practical Photographer* described him as holding 'one of the highest positions as an exponent of portraiture.' His

CW   *Camera Work*
DKP   *Die Kunst in der Photographie*
GIE   Glasgow International Exhibition
LR   Linked Ring
PS   Photo-Secession

sitters included Andrew Carnegie and Sir Robert Rowand Anderson. 1901 exhibited at the GIE.

GEORGE DAVISON
1856–1930
Worked in England. 1892 founder member of the LR. 1898 Managing Director, Kodak in Britain. Published in CW. 1901 exhibited at the GIE. Worked in gum, platinum and photogravure. 1911 leader of the group which formed the London Secession. His *An Old Farmstead* (re-named *The Onion Field*) shown at the Royal Photographic Society in 1890 is an early, key work in Pictorial Photography.

F. HOLLAND DAY
1864–1933
Worked in the U.S.A. Member of the LR. Published in DKP. 1896–1898 made a series of photographs on *The Passion of Christ*. 1900 the Royal Photographic Society showed Day's exhibition 'The New School of American Photography'. 1901 exhibited at the GIE. 1902 'Portraits by a Few Leaders in the Newer Photographic Methods' mounted in Day's studio in Boston included Annan, Coburn, Demachy, Evans, Käsebier and White.

ROBERT DEMACHY
1859–1936
Worked in France. 1894 founder member of the Photo-Club de Paris. Member of the LR. Published in CW and in DKP. Worked in gum-bichromate. 1897 published with Alfred Maskell *Photo-Aquatint, or the Gum Bichromate Process*. 1901 exhibited at the GIE. 1905 awarded Legion of Honour. 1907 published his defence of *l'intervention* in 'The Straight and the Modified Print', *The Amateur Photographer*, 22 Jan. 1907. 1936 presented *In a Garden Fair* by Annan to the Royal Photographic Society.

PETER HENRY EMERSON
1856–1936
Worked in England. 1886 with T. F. Goodall published *Life and Landscape in the Norfolk Broads* illustrated with 40 platinotypes, one of a

number of photographically illustrated books, the last, *Marsh Leaves*, in 1895. Published his theories in *Naturalistic Photography for Students of the Art*, 1889 (which is claimed to have inaugurated Pictorialism) and then refuted them in *Death of Naturalistic Photography*, 1890.

FRANK EUGENE
1865–1936
Worked in the U.S.A. and Germany. Painter and photographer. Founder member of the PS. Member of the LR. Published in CW. Manipulated his negatives with an etching needle. Worked in autochrome. 1901 exhibited at the GIE. 1906 settled permanently in Germany. 1913 Professor of Pictorial Photography, Royal Academy of Graphic Arts, Leipzig, the first appointment of this kind.

FREDERICK H. EVANS
1853–1943
Worked in England. Member of the LR. Published in CW and in DKP. 1901 exhibited at the GIE. 1902–05 decorated and hung the London Salon. 1906 a group of his cathedral studies comprised with Annan's and Hill and Adamson's work, the 'First Exhibition of British Photography' in Stieglitz's 291 Gallery, New York. A purist, in that he did not manipulate his negatives. 1937 gifted to the Royal Photographic Society *Harlech Castle, Stirling Castle* and *The Ox Cart* by Annan.

SADAKICHI HARTMANN
1867–1944
Worked in the U.S.A. Japanese-German writer. A prolific photographic critic and champion of photography as an art form. For a selection of his writings (and a bibliography) see Hartmann *The Valiant Knights of Daguerre*, Lawson and Knox (eds.), University of California Press, 1978.

PAUL HAVILAND
1880–1950
Worked in the U.S.A. Member of the PS. Photographs and writings published in CW. 1913 published with Marius de Zayas *A Study of the*

Modern Evolution of Plastic Expression. 1916 returned to Limoges in his native France.

DAVID OCTAVIUS HILL
1802–1870
and
ROBERT ADAMSON
1821–1848
Worked in Scotland. Hill, a painter, and Adamson, Scotland's first professional photographer in the calotype process, joined in partnership in 1843. Their association ended with Adamson's death in 1848. The photographs they took were remarkable for their range of invention and skill and set a standard for future photography not just in Scotland. Annan promoted their almost forgotten work by lending his carbon and photogravure prints from their negatives to exhibitions in Europe and America. In 1906 Stieglitz's 291 Gallery, New York, showed a group of one original and seventeen Annan prints. The catalogue hailed Hill and Adamson's photographs as 'pioneer pictorial photographic work' and stated that the portraits with their 'powerful characterization and artistic quality have never been surpassed.' Published, posthumously, in CW.

ALFRED HORSLEY HINTON
1863–1908
Worked in England. Founder member of the LR. Published in CW and in DKP. From 1893 until his death edited *The Amateur Photographer.* 1898 published *Practical Pictorial Photography.* 1899 organised British section of the Philadelphia Photographic Salon. 1901 exhibited at the GIE. 1904 supervised the exhibition of British photographs at the St Louis Exposition at which Annan acted as a member of the jury.

THEODOR HOFMEISTER
1865–1943
and
OSKAR HOFMEISTER
1869–1937
The Hofmeister Brothers worked in Germany. Members of *Die Gesellschaft zur Förderung der Amateur-Photographie,* Hamburg and of the LR.

Worked in gum-bichromate. Published in CW and in DKP. 1901 exhibited at the GIE. Latterly Oskar made the exposures, Theodor printed.

FREDERICK HOLLYER
1838–1933
Worked in England. Member of the LR. Published in DKP. A specialist in the reproduction of works of art including the paintings of G. F. Watts. Portraiture included William Morris and John Ruskin.

EMILE OTTO HOPPÉ
1878–1972
Worked in England. Portrait and travel photographer. 1922 published *Fair Women* and 1934 *Travels Round the World with a Camera.* Published in DKP.

ERNST JUHL
1850–1915
Worked in Germany. Founded *Die Gesellschaft zur Förderung der Amateur-Photographie.* As suggested by Alfred Lichtwark, organised annual exhibitions of photography at the Kunsthalle, Hamburg 1893–1903. Corresponded with Annan over the loan of Hill and Adamson prints to an exhibition in 1899. After his death his collection was split between Berlin and Hamburg. The Staatliche Museen Preussischer Kulturbesitz, Berlin acquired nine of his Annans with some Annan prints from Hill and Adamson.

GERTRUDE KÄSEBIER
1852–1934
Worked in the U.S.A. Founder member of the PS. 1900 first woman to be elected to the LR. 1897 opened a portrait studio in New York. Published in CW and in DKP. 1901 exhibited at the GIE. 1910 President of the Women's Federation of the Professional Photographers Association of America. 1912 resigned from the PS after a difference of opinion with Stieglitz.

JOSEPH T. KEILY
1869–1914
Worked in the U.S.A. Founder member of the PS. Member of the LR. 1901 exhibited at the GIE. Photographs and articles published in CW, including one in October 1904 on Annan, whom he referred to as 'one of the foremost artists in photography, not only in England, but of the world.'

HEINRICH KUEHN
1866–1944
Worked in Austria. Member of the Vienna Camera Club, the LR and the PS. Published in CW and in DKP. 1896 with Henneberg and Watzek formed *Das Kleeblatt*. 1901 exhibited at the GIE. 1912 founded a school of art photography in Innsbruck.

MAX LEHRS
Worked in Germany. Director of the Kupferstich-Kabinett, Dresden. 1899 formed one of the earliest collections of photography in a public institution. 1900 acquired Annan's *Woman with Hat*.

ALFRED LICHTWARK
1852–1914
Worked in Germany. Director of the Kunsthalle, Hamburg. An early supporter of a museum of photography. 1894 published *Die Bedeutung der Amateur-Photographie*.

FRITZ MATTHIES-MASUREN
Worked in Germany. Writer, organiser and champion of Pictorialism. 1898 wrote introduction to the catalogue of the *Internationalen Elite-Ausstellung Künstlerische Photographien*, Munich. The aim of this exhibition, which included Annan, was 'to win respect for photography as an independent artistic medium.' 1907 published *Künstlerische Photographie*. The Staatliche Museen Preussischer Kulturbesitz, Berlin hold four Annans once in his collection.

ALEXIS MAZOURINE
Worked in Russia, Austria and Germany. Published in DKP. 1901 exhibited at the GIE.

FRANCIS H. NEWBERY
1855–1946
Worked in Scotland. Because he was Director of the Glasgow School of Art and involved with C. R. Mackintosh in its new building, Newbery's activities as a photographer have been overlooked. Exhibited at the London Salon. 1901 exhibited at the GIE. Painted a portrait of Annan now in the possession of the School.

MUNGO PONTON
1802–1880
Worked in Scotland. Lawyer and banker. Amateur scientist who discovered the chemistry of the carbon process which he published in 1839. Author of what may be the only known hymn referring to photography.

CONSTANT PUYO
1857–1933
Worked in France. Member of the *Photo-Club de Paris* and the LR. Published in CW and in DKP. Made highly-manipulated gum bichromate prints. 1901 exhibited at the GIE. 1906 published with Demachy *Les Procédés d'Art en Photographie*.

OSCAR REJLANDER
1813–1875
Worked in England. 1857 showed his controversial, large, composite *Two Ways of Life* at Manchester. His photographs paved the way, to some extent, for Pictorialism.

HENRY PEACH ROBINSON
1830–1901
Worked in England. Founder member of the LR. Published in DKP. 1869 published *Pictorial Effect in Photography* which was translated into French and German and had a profound influence. Used combination printing for his carefully constructed figure compositions, some from literary sources.

GEORGE BERNARD SHAW
1856–1950
Worked in England. Writer and dramatist. From about 1885 wrote photographic criticism.

For his views on photography see *Wilson's Photographic Magazine*, vol.56, 1909. Practised photography. Published one print in cw, a portrait of Alvin Langdon Coburn.

EDWARD STEICHEN
1879–1973
Worked in the U.S.A. and France. Painter and photographer. Declined invitation to join the LR. 1901 exhibited at the GIE. Founder member of the PS. Published in DKP and in cw for which he designed the cover. 1902 exhibited his paintings and photographs in Paris. 1920 concentrated solely on photography. 1923 photographed for *Vogue* and *Vanity Fair*. 1947 Director, Department of Photography, Museum of Modern Art, New York. 1955 organised the influential exhibition 'The Family of Man'. Steichen wrote about Annan as 'one whom we have been taught to look up to' in *Camera Notes*, January 1901.

ALFRED STIEGLITZ
1864–1946
Worked in the U.S.A. Photographer and impresario. An exact contemporary of J. Craig Annan. Member of the LR. Founder member of the PS. 1897–1902 edited *Camera Notes*. 1901 exhibited at the GIE. 1902–17 edited *Camera Work*. Published in cw and in DKP. 1905 with help of Steichen founded the Little Galleries of the Photo-Secession at 291 Fifth Avenue, New York, which, as well as photography, showed the work of Rodin, Cézanne, Brancusi and Picasso. The Metropolitan Museum of Modern Art acquired a collection of photographs from his collection which included forty-five prints by Annan.

FRANK MEADOW SUTCLIFFE
1853–1941
Worked in England. Professional portrait photographer who also recorded the disappearing life of fisherfolk at Whitby. Member of the LR. Published in DKP. 1901 exhibited at the GIE.

JAMES VALENTINE
1815–80
Worked in Scotland. The Valentine company was founded as a printing firm in 1825 in Dundee by James's father. The firm turned to photography in the 1850s. It produced well-known views for the tourist trade, eventually dominating the picture postcard market. Archive in St Andrews University.

CLARENCE H. WHITE
1871–1925
Worked in the U.S.A. 1898 helped found the Newark Camera Club, met Day, Käsebier, Keily and Stieglitz at Philadelphia. 1899 showed at the LR. 1900 elected LR. 1901 exhibited at the GIE. 1902 founder member of the PS. Published in cw. 1908–21 instructor of photography, Brooklyn Institute of Arts and Sciences. 1914 founded the Clarence H. White School of Photography, New York. 1916 elected first President of the Pictorial Photographers of America.

GEORGE WASHINGTON WILSON
1823–93
Worked in Scotland. The head of a huge commercial photographic enterprise founded *c.*1855 in Aberdeen producing views from all over Europe sometimes at a rate of about 5,000 prints a day. 1859 his *Princes Street, Edinburgh* is the first instantaneous street view to be published in Britain. Archive in Aberdeen University.

ANNAN'S CIRCLE OF FRIENDS

SIR D. Y. CAMERON, R.S.A., R.A., R.S.W., R.W.S., R.E., LL.D.
1865–1945
Worked in Scotland and England. Etcher and painter. An early influence from Annan is Cameron's etching *Old Age* 1891, a re-working of Hill and Adamson's *Mrs Rigby*. Travelled in Europe. Produced landscapes and architectural

subjects. Trustee of the National Gallery and the National Gallery of Scotland. Honorary Degrees from Cambridge, Glasgow and Manchester. 1912 Annan lent two works by Cameron *St Mark's Venice* and *Street in Cairo* from his collection to Dundee. 1933 King's Painter and Limner in Scotland.

J. PITTENDRIGH MCGILLIVRAY, R.S.A., LL.D.

1856–1938

Worked in Scotland. Sole sculptor of the 'Glasgow Boys'. Public sculpture includes Byron in Aberdeen, Burns in Irvine and Gladstone and figures on the Scottish National Portrait Gallery in Edinburgh. 1921 King's Sculptor in Ordinary for Scotland. Also interested in poetry and photography. 1930 published 'The Art of Photography', *The Photographic Journal*, January.

WILLIAM STRANG, R.A., LL.D.

1859–1921

Worked in England. Etcher and painter. 1880 founder member of the Royal Society of Painter Etchers. 1895 joined Art Workers Guild. 1918 President of the International Society of Sculptors, Painters & Engravers. Made portrait engravings, often from life, including G. Bernard Shaw and the sculptor, Sir George Frampton, both of whom also sat for Annan.

GEORGE WALTON

1868–1933

Worked in Scotland and England. 1888 opened a interior decoration and design firm in Glasgow. Annan took a few shares in 1897 when it became a limited company. 1897 moved to London where George Davison gave him commissions for Kodak. Began to design complete buildings, the best of which is, perhaps, The Leys, Elstree, 1901, for John B. B. Wellington a photographer, member of the LR and manager of the Kodak works at Harrow. 1903 designed the cover for *The Practical Photographer*. Published in *Decorative Kunst* and championed by Muthesius.

COLOPHON

This book has been designed by Robert Dalrymple
and typeset on Monotype equipment similar to that
in use in Annan's lifetime.

The text typeface is Old Style No.2, cut in 1901 by
Monotype after the designs of Miller & Richard, the
Edinburgh type foundry; the display face is
Gloucester Old Style, dating from 1896.

The setting was carried out by Harry McIntosh at
Speedspools in Edinburgh using his unique
Mactronic program to work from the author's
word-processed disk.

The book has been printed by BAS Printers of Over
Wallop on Stockbridge Wove 115gsm and Parilux
Matt 150gsm papers.

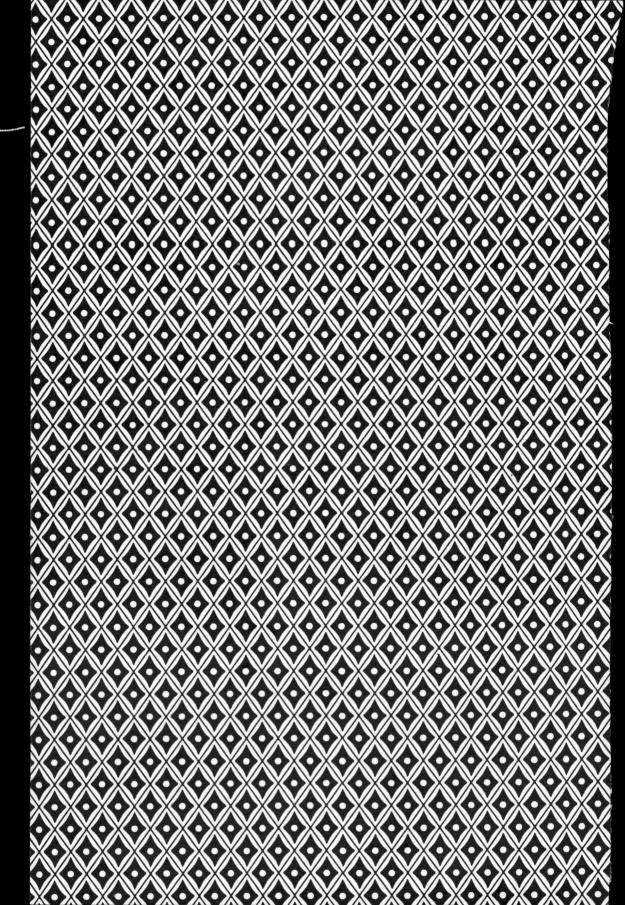

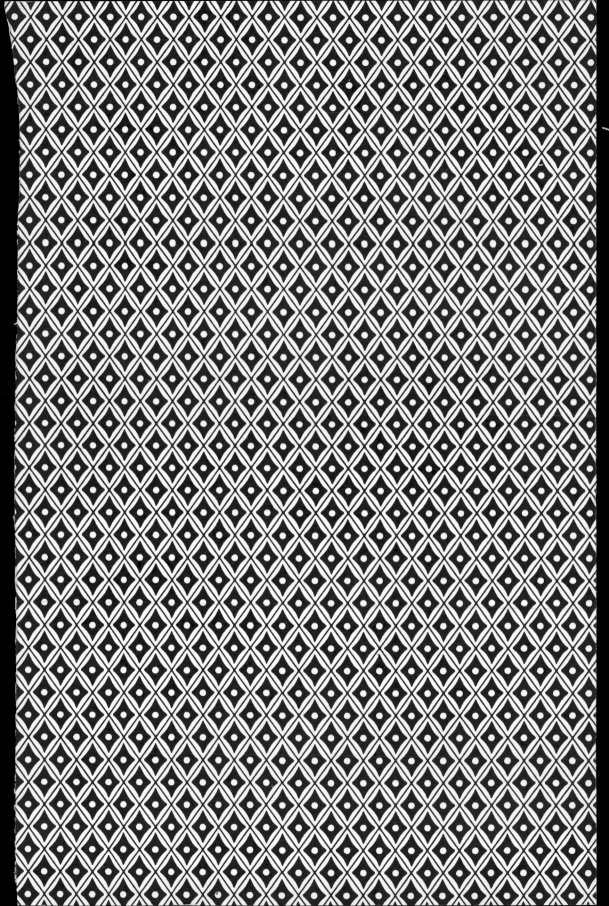